ALL ABOUT SMALL BOATS

JUSTINE CIOVACCO

Britannica®
Educational Publishing

IN ASSOCIATION WITH

ROSEN
EDUCATIONAL SERVICES

Published in 2017 by Britannica Educational Publishing (a trademark of Encyclopædia Britannica, Inc.) in association with The Rosen Publishing Group, Inc.
29 East 21st Street, New York, NY 10010

Distributed exclusively by Rosen Publishing.
To see additional Britannica Educational Publishing titles, go to rosenpublishing.com.

First Edition

Britannica Educational Publishing
J.E. Luebering: Executive Director, Core Editorial
Mary Rose McCudden: Editor, Britannica Student Encyclopedia

Rosen Publishing
Christine Poolos: Editor
Nelson Sá: Art Director
Nicole Russo: Designer
Cindy Reiman: Photography Manager
Sherri Jackson: Photo Researcher

Library of Congress Cataloging-in-Publication Data

Names: Ciovacco, Justine, author.
Title: All about small boats / Justine Ciovacco.
Description: First edition. | New York : Britannica Educational Publishing in association with Rosen Educational Services, [2017] | Series: Let's find out! Transportation | Includes bibliographical references and index. | Audience: 1-4.
Identifiers: LCCN 2015051444| ISBN 9781680484441 (library bound : alk. paper)
| ISBN 9781680484526 (pbk. : alk. paper) | ISBN 9781680484212 (6-pack : alk. paper)
Subjects: LCSH: Boats and boating—Juvenile literature.
Classification: LCC GV775.3 .C56 2017 | DDC 797.1—dc23
LC record available at http://lccn.loc.gov/2015051444

Photo credits: Cover, p. 1 serenarossi/Shutterstock.com; p. 4 Kzenon/Shutterstock.com; p. 5 Oleksiy Maksymenko/All Canada Photos/Getty Images; p. 6 Buyenlarge/Archive Photos/Getty Images; p. 7 © imageBroker/Alamy Stock Photo; p. 8 © PhotoAlto sas/ Alamy Stock Photo; p. 9 Mike Clarke/iStock/Thinkstock; p. 10 Jordi C/Shutterstock.com; p. 11 John Kropewnicki/Shutterstock. com; p. 12 Michael Blann/Photodisc/Thinkstock; p. 13 Darryl Brooks/Shutterstock.com; pp. 14, 16 Encyclopedia Britannica, Inc.; p. 15 Goodluz/Shutterstock.com; p.17 Alison Langley/Photolibrary/Getty Images; p. 18 Alessio Moiola/Shutterstock.com; p. 19 ©iStockphoto.com/walkingwounded; p. 20 Creatas Images/Thinkstock; p. 21 Image Source/Photodisc/Getty Images; p. 22 Ken Taylor/ iStock/Thinkstock; p. 23 Imfoto/Shutterstock.com; p. 24 Ralf Siemieniec/iStock/Thinkstock; p. 25 Alvov/Shutterstock.com; p. 26 Patryk Kosmider/Shutterstock.com; p. 27 Coast Guard Public/SuperStock; p. 28 Noel Hendrickson/The Image Bank/Getty Images; p. 29 ThomasEdwards77/iStock/Thinkstock; interior pages background image In Green/Shutterstock.com

CONTENTS

Boats Afloat

Riding in a rowboat is a relaxing way to enjoy nature.

People have used boats to move goods and people across water for thousands of years. Today, the word *boat* means a small water vessel used for fun, for travel, or for carrying small loads. They are different than large vessels that carry many people or goods. Those are called ships.

Small boats allow people to travel by water without getting wet. They help people get to work, and some people, like fishermen, actually work on boats. Small boats are also perfect for exploring and getting from place to place. Many people enjoy taking a canoe, rowboat, or kayak out on a river or a small lake. On larger or rougher bodies of water, motorboats and sailboats are used for recreation.

Small boats can be powered by people, by sails, or by motors. They are a diverse group. How they look depends on what they are used for.

Diverse means different from each other.

Many people enjoy waterskiing and other water sports using small boats.

EARLY BOATS

Ancient peoples used boats as many as ten thousand years ago. Most of the earliest boats were just canoes made from hollow logs. Others were flat rafts made of reeds, logs, or grass tied together. Examples of these early boats have been found in India, Egypt, Mexico, Peru, and Bolivia, among other places.

This boat was made from a bull's skin stretched over a wood frame.

Some early boats were also made from animal skins stretched over a wood frame. Examples of this are seen in Inuit and Native American kayaks. Sometimes people

Vikings had large and small boats. This Viking sailboat is at a museum in Norway.

also used tree bark to make the boats strong.

Early boats were mainly used to carry materials. For example, ancient Egyptian carvings show that the stones used to make the pyramids were moved, in part, by boats.

Early sailboats were used by Scandinavian explorers beginning in about 600 CE. People called Vikings used boats with sails made of wool to help them cross the Atlantic Ocean more than one thousand years ago.

COMPARE AND CONTRAST

Early Native Americans used animal skins, while Egyptians used reeds to make boats. Why might they have chosen these boat materials?

TURNING THE TIDE

By the mid-1800s, people were building boats out of wooden planks. Many boats even had iron or steel frames. Boatmakers added tall poles called masts and attached fabric sails to the masts to catch the wind. Later, people added engines for speed.

Boating for fun and sport became popular in the mid-1900s. One reason for this was that boat materials were

Sails don't have to be fancy. This man in India made one using many pieces of cloth.

Aluminum is a lightweight material. This aluminum boat can move quickly through the water.

becoming easier to produce then. This made boats cheaper and easier for people to buy. The addition of motors made boats easier to control.

Aluminum is now a popular material for small boats. It does not rust or break down in salt water as many other materials do. Another popular material is fiberglass, which is a mix of plastic and glass. Modern boat materials are also coated with chemicals and human-made materials to stay strong in rough waters.

Think About It

The earliest boats did not have motors or sails. How would those have helped ancient people?

Boats, Boats Everywhere

The kinds of boats we use today are as different as the rivers, lakes, and seas on which we travel. In general, boats can be grouped into three main kinds. The groups are based on the type of power needed to move them through the water: people, sails, and motors.

Many boats need only the effort of human muscles to move them. Canoes and kayaks are small, lightweight boats with pointed ends. People use paddles to move canoes and kayaks.

People use paddles to make kayaks move. Powering a kayak through water takes a lot of muscle.

A team of rowers working together, called a crew, gives this boat enough power and speed to race against others.

Rowboats are wider and heavier than canoes. People move rowboats forward with long poles called oars.

It takes a lot of energy to move a boat. One person can row alone, but people rowing together help move a boat faster—as long as they all row at the same time and in the same direction!

THINK ABOUT IT

Everyone in a small boat must try to row in the same direction. What would happen if they didn't?

Sailboats are boats with sails. These large pieces of cloth are raised on tall posts called masts. Sails catch the wind, which pushes a sailboat along. Sailboats range in size from small, one-person boats to huge sailing ships that can cross oceans.

A motorboat is any boat powered by a motor. Engines can be inboard or outboard. An inboard engine is permanently mounted inside the boat. An outboard engine is clamped to the outside of a boat's frame and can

The sails on a sailboat can be moved to make the boat go in different directions.

A cabin cruiser is a large motorboat. It has enough space for people to walk around, relax, and enjoy the view.

be removed easily. Both types usually move the boat by turning a propeller in the water.

Motorboats, like sailboats, can range greatly in size. Small motorboats are simple, hollow vessels. Larger motorboats include cabin cruisers. These boats can have living areas including kitchens and bunks (beds) for several people.

COMPARE AND CONTRAST

Sailboats are usually harder to control than motorboats. What makes sailboats harder to control?

Parts of a Boat

No matter what their size, most boats have several common parts. The hull is the body, or frame, of the boat. The walls of the boat are called bulkheads. The deck is the floor of the boat.

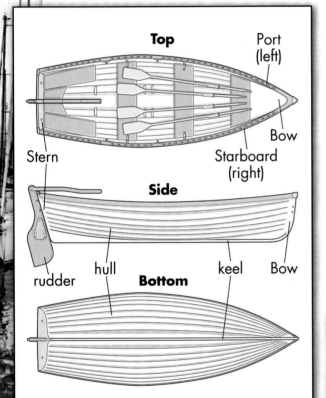

Top
Port (left)
Bow
Starboard (right)
Stern

Side
hull
keel
Bow

Bottom
rudder

The keel and the rudder are under the boat. The keel runs from the front to the back. It sticks into the water to keep the boat from tipping over sideways. The rudder is attached to the back of the boat. It is a flat, smooth piece of wood or metal that is used to steer the boat.

Boats are designed to stay afloat and to move through the water. Most have the same basic parts.

◀◀

Sailboats have additional parts. Sails are raised and lowered on the mast. The boom anchors the sail.

The sections of boats also have special names. The front of the boat is called the bow. The back is called the stern. The left side of the boat is called port. The right side is called starboard.

THINK ABOUT IT

Larger boats that carry many people or tons of goods over long distances are called ships. How are ships different than smaller boats?

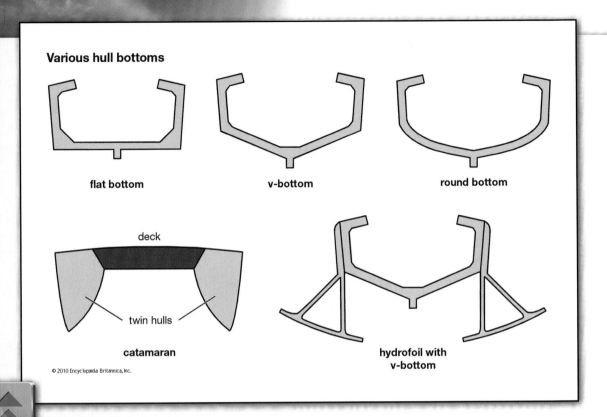

Various hull bottoms

flat bottom

v-bottom

round bottom

deck

twin hulls

catamaran

© 2010 Encyclopædia Britannica, Inc.

hydrofoil with
v-bottom

Hulls come in a variety of designs to suit different waters.

The shape of a sailboat hull is designed to fit how a boat will be used and the kind of waters in which it will be sailed. A flat hull is common for boats moving on small bodies of water. A deeper hull is necessary in deeper waters because the waters out in the middle of the ocean are usually rougher.

Small sailboats, like this dinghy, can stay afloat in rough waters because they have a deep hull.

Engines are machines that use the energy of steam, gas, or oil to provide power to something.

Catboats have a single mast and one sail. Most catboats and other small sailboats usually have a centerboard or a dagger board to provide stability and to minimize tipping. These boards can be raised and lowered through the center of the boat. The keel does this in larger boats.

Motorboats have a different hull. They also have engines, but the engine is in different places on different kinds of motorboats. For example, speedboats have a motor set within the hull.

WHATEVER FLOATS YOUR BOAT

Some boats are still made of wood. This Italian shipyard builds wooden boats.

The earliest boats were made of hollowed reeds or trees with their insides carved out. The fact that the materials were not solid is important. This made them lighter so they could float.

Wood is still used to make some boats. Today, the wood is usually in flat, wide boards called planks. The wood is smoothed and designed to create frames that can easily move through water. Most modern boats are made from fiberglass or aluminum. Fiberglass is a material made from tiny pieces of glass combined with plastic, while aluminum is a light metal. The weight of a boat and how it is made help explain why it floats. Boats float if they weigh less than the maximum amount of water they can push aside.

Boats don't always stay afloat! This man's boat is taking on water, which will make it sink.

MAKING BOATS MOVE

Different small boats have different tools to make them move. Most need at least a bit of human help.

Rowboats and canoes have at least one person using poles called paddles or oars to move the boat. Two people with oars can help these boats move faster. Larger rowboats may have four or eight people all rowing at the same time!

The sail on a sailboat catches the wind. This makes the boat move in the direction the wind blows. However,

A girl uses a set of oars to propel a rowboat through the water.

people are needed to lift, lower, and change the direction of the sails. People guide sailboats.

Motorboats, including speedboats, are just like cars. They need a person to start and stop the engine. Of course, a person is also needed to guide the boat. Some boats have motors that can be moved to change the direction of the boat.

THINK ABOUT IT

People need licenses to drive cars and boats. What kinds of things should people learn before driving a boat?

This boat has an outboard engine. It is clamped to the outside of the hull and is easily removed.

GONE WITH THE WIND

A sailboat is just a boat if it does not have a sail. Sails are the large pieces of fabric that catch the wind. Wind blowing against the boat at an angle fills the sail. That makes the fabric puff out and helps push the boat forward. People often move the sails by hand or, in modern times, by computer while sailing. This makes the boat change direction.

The sails are not the only boat parts that make sailing possible. The keel is a long,

A sailboat's sails are used to catch the wind. Wind pushes against the sails to help make the ship move.

An upside-down boat shows a broken keel. The keel is needed to help the boat stay on top of the water.

thin piece that sticks down from the bottom of the boat. This piece helps the boat to balance as it is pushed along by the wind. A sailboat would fall sideways if the keel didn't hold it upright.

THINK ABOUT IT

A boat must travel at an angle to the wind in order to sail faster. Why does the angle affect the boat's speed?

Racing on the Water

Not all boats move *in* the water. Hydrofoil boats move on its surface. These are among the fastest boats, with speeds as high as 60 to 70 miles (100 to 110 kilometers) per hour. That's as fast as a car on a highway!

Hydrofoils start moving with their hull in the water. Wing-shaped parts called

A hydrofoil glides on top of the water. Its foils lift the boat out of the water as its speed increases.

foils that are under the water help raise the boat up when it reaches a certain speed.

Some sailboats and rowboats are also used for speed. Very narrow rowboats called shells or sculls are used in the sport of racing. Several categories of rowing are events in the Olympic Games. Sailboats and motorboats are also used for racing. The most famous international sailing competition is the America's Cup race.

THINK ABOUT IT

Since airplane travel is faster than ocean travel, why would anyone sail to their destination?

Sailboats can move with great speed. These sailboats are racing against each other in a regatta.

25

Boats Get Down to Business

Boats are important tools for the work of many people. These include fishermen and members of life-saving groups, such as the U.S. Coast Guard.

Fishermen use different kinds of boats. Rowboats may be used in calm waters. The sound of a motor would scare the fish away! Small motorboats with cabins are better for fishermen who need to move deeper out to sea. They can quickly go to deeper parts of the ocean to drop

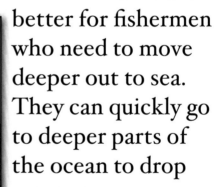

Greek fishermen search for fish on a small boat in the middle of the sea.

nets to catch fish, shrimp, and other sea animals used for food.

Tugboats are also small working boats. They help guide large ships into and out of ports. They push or pull ships that are too large to make small turns on their own.

The U.S. Coast Guard protects people in the water. They use helicopters and boats to patrol the country's coastline. They help people whose boats have capsized or who are in need of assistance.

A Coast Guard boat searches for people who need help in the water.

Capsized means to be overturned.

WATER WORLD

Small boats have been used for work and pleasure since ancient times. The materials used to make boats have changed, but the earliest boats worked the same way as boats today. A structure that floats holds people while moving over water.

Different kinds of paddles, sails, foils, engines, and other parts help boats move. Still, people are needed to guide most boats.

Boats help us to explore the world from the water. Large

A pontoon boat provides a steady place from which many people can wait for fish.

Boats enable people to move through the water and enjoy nature's beauty from a different perspective.

ships carried the earliest explorers to new lands, but smaller boats helped the explorers follow rivers farther into those lands. Today, tour boats continue to allow people to learn new things about the world around them. The many different kinds of boats available today give people choices. Different types can help them work, travel, or just enjoy their free time.

THINK ABOUT IT

Where can small boats go that large ships cannot?

GLOSSARY

aluminum A lightweight silver-white material that conducts electricity and heat well and does not rust easily.

cabin A small room on a boat for passengers or crew.

canoe A long light narrow boat with pointed ends and curved sides that is usually moved by someone using a paddle.

clamped Fastened or tightened.

fiberglass Glass in the form of fibers used in making various products, such as yarn, insulation, or boats.

frame An arrangement of parts that gives form or support to something.

guide Something that leads or directs another on course.

hollow An empty space within something.

hydrofoil A boat that has fins or wing-shaped parts attached to the bottom by braces for lifting the hull clear out of the water to allow faster speeds.

kayak A type of canoe that is covered, except for an opening in the middle where the paddler or paddlers sit.

oar A long pole with a broad blade at one end used for rowing or steering a boat.

paddle An instrument with a flat blade to move and steer a small boat.

planks Wide, thick boards.

raft A flat structure (such as a group of logs fastened together) for support or transportation on water.

rowboat A small boat rowed, or moved, by oars.

sailboat A boat with fabric sails.

solid Filled throughout; not hollow.

steer To guide or direct the course of.

vessel A craft used for navigating in water; usually used for a craft bigger than a rowboat.

FOR MORE INFORMATION

Books

Biggs, Brian. *Everything Goes: By Sea.* New York, NY: Balzer + Bray, 2013.

Lyon, George Ella. *Boats Float!* New York, NY: Atheneum/Richard Jackson Book, 2015.

Oxlade, Chris. *Stickmen's Guide to Watercraft* (Stickmen's Guide to How Everything Works). Minneapolis, MN: Hungry Tomato, 2016.

Thomas, Isabel. *First Book of Ships and Boats.* London, UK: A & C Black, 2014.

Websites

Because of the changing nature of Internet links, Rosen Publishing has developed an online list of websites related to the subject of this book. This site is updated regularly. Please use this link to access this list:

http://www.rosenlinks.com/LFO/sboat

INDEX